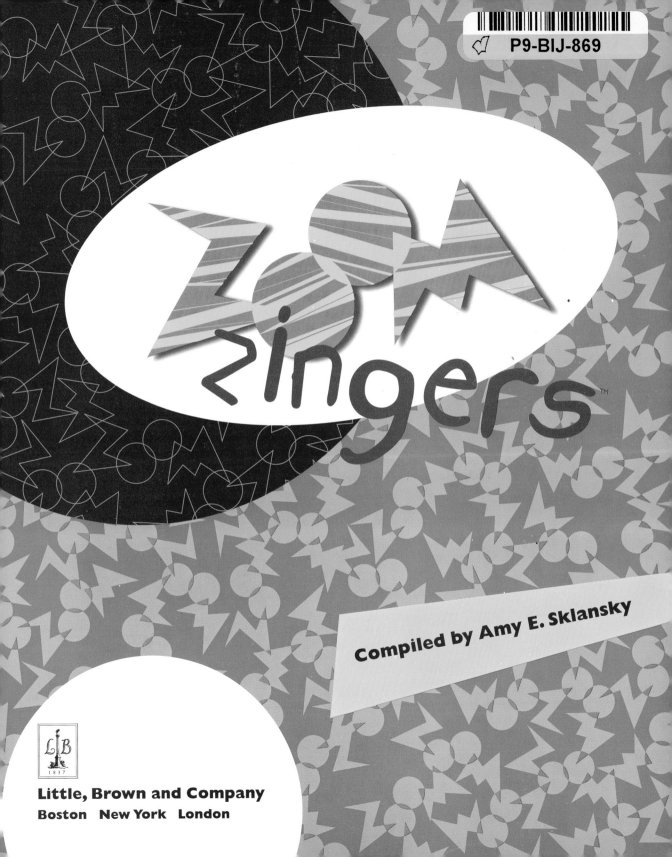

Zoo Zingers™

Compiled by Amy E. Sklansky

Little, Brown and Company
Boston   New York   London

First Edition

ZOOM, ZOOMzingers, ZOOMfun, ZOOMerang, ZOOMa Cum Laude, ZOOMmedia, and all composite ZOOM marks contained herein are trademarks of the WGBH Educational Foundation.

Library of Congress Cataloging-in-Publication Data

Sklansky, Amy E.
    ZOOMzingers / compiled by Amy E. Sklansky — 1st ed.
        p.   cm.
    Summary: A collection of brainteasers, physical challenges, jokes, word games, number games, and card tricks inspired by the television show ZOOM. Features a behind-the-scenes peek at what goes into filming an episode of ZOOM.
    ISBN 0-316-95261-3
    1. Games — Juvenile literature.   2. Card tricks — Juvenile literature.   3. Word games — Juvenile literature.   4. Number games — Juvenile literature.   5. ZOOM (Television program : WGBH (Television station : Boston, Mass.)) — Juvenile literature. [1. Games. 2. Word games. 3. Number games.] I. ZOOM (Television program : WGBH (Television station : Boston, Mass.)) II. Title. III. Title: ZOOMzingers.
    GV1203.S56   1999
    793.7 — dc21   99-11684

10 9 8 7 6 5 4 3 2 1

Q-KPT
Printed in the United States of America

Funding for ZOOM is provided by
public television viewers,
the National Science Foundation,
and the Corporation for Public Broadcasting.

Design by WGBH

Hey, ZOOMers™

ZOOM™ is TV by kids, for kids.™ **Without you,** there wouldn't be a show! Everything you see on ZOOM was sent in by kids from all over the country.

Each show is a **cool mix** of games, experiments, crafts, kid guests, recipes, brainteasers, jokes, skits, and more. After watching, you'll want to try all the activities yourself.

But ZOOM is more than TV. We have a Web site at **www.pbs.org/zoom** and our own newsletter called ZOOMerang.™ So check us out when you're surfing the Internet. Send us your ideas by mail or e-mail, and we'll send you the latest edition of ZOOMerang and consider putting your ideas on the show.

For now, though, turn the page to find body-challenging, mind-boggling **ZOOMzingers,**™ jokes, Ubbi Dubbi™ commercials, wacky facts, and more. You might recognize some of your favorite things from the show, but you'll find lots of new stuff, too, including a peek at what goes on behind the scenes at ZOOM. We dare you to read this book without getting zingered! Put your **body and brain to the test,** ZOOMers!

Alisa   Keiko   Jared   Zoe   Pablo

David   Lynese

P.S. **Check out** the last page to find out how to send your ideas to ZOOM.

1

Contents

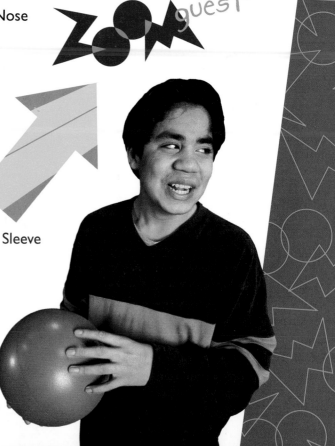

ZOOMguest™

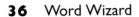

whatZup!

Hubappuby rubeadubing!

What? You can't understand what I'm saying? That's because I'm speaking Ubbi Dubbi, ZOOM's secret language. We promise to reveal the secret to speaking Ubbi Dubbi before this book ends, so keep reading!

Everything You Ever Wanted to Know about ZOOM

Bend your elbow so that your hand (palm up) rests near your shoulder.

Put a penny on your forearm near your elbow.

Can you **extend** your arm quickly and catch the penny with that same hand? You'll have to be quick or you'll be in a "Penny Pinch."

P.S. If you can do this, try it with more than one penny.

Penny Pinch

Zfact:

According to the Guinness Book of Records 1996, the coin snatching record is 328 out of 482 British 10-pence coins (roughly the same size and weight as an American quarter). The record-holder spent 20 minutes stacking the coins into 13 linked columns. He says, "The **wider** the stack, the **better**, provided it's within your hand span."

Zoops

"My most embarrassing moment is when my dad starts acting like an animal in front of me."
— Vanessa E. of Mora, Minnesota

Run, Rabbit, Run

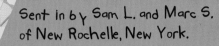
Sent in by Sam L. and Marc S. of New Rochelle, New York.

Put a pencil under your nose.

Then **put** your hands behind your back.

Say "Run, rabbit, run" as many times as you can without dropping the pencil.

How many times can you do it? Have a contest with a friend.

P.S. Try saying it faster!

If you think this zinger is easy, try substituting any of these tricky tongue twisters for "Run, rabbit, run." Good luck!

A big black bear babbled to a bored bald bat till the bored bald bat bawled.

Sweet sheep sleep soundly on shiny sheets.

5

You will need a ball and a jump rope.

- Place the ball between your knees.

- Ask two friends to turn the rope.

- Now try to jump rope without dropping the ball.

- Count how many jumps you can do before dropping the ball. Then challenge a friend and see who can get the most jumps.

Sent in by Michael H. of Larchmont, New York.

Jump Rope
CHALLENGE

zfact:
According to the *Guinness Book of Records 1996*, the record for the most turns of a jump rope is **14,628.**

The Language of Jump Rope

If you'd like to do some more jumping, here are some terms you might want to know:

high water = don't let the rope touch the ground as it turns

mustard and vinegar = turn the rope at normal speed

pepper = turn the rope as quickly as you can

rocking the cradle or blue bells = swing the rope from side to side only

salt = turn the rope slowly

Feather Float

Sent in by Ed L. of Marblehead, Massachusetts.

See how long you and your friends can keep a feather up in the air without touching it.

The catch is that the same person can't blow the feather twice in a row.

Hint: Try blowing or waving your hands underneath the feather.

z fact:

The Japanese Phoenix Fowl has tail feathers that are longer than a giraffe is tall. The longest feather ever measured was **more than 34 feet** in length! Maybe you shouldn't use one of these feathers for this zinger!

z oops!

"My most embarrassing moment was when I was three. I was walking along and my pants fell down and everyone started laughing and I didn't notice. And so I looked down and I noticed that my pants were off and I was wearing Barney underwear."

— Emily K. of Rocky River, Ohio

According to the Guinness Book of Records 1996, the largest container of popcorn held **6,619.76 cubic feet** of popcorn. It was almost **40 feet** long, more than **20 feet** wide, and **8 feet** high.

Think about how many movies that tub of popcorn would last you!

Here's a **joke** from Sarah H. of Orlando, Florida:

What's fluffy, white, and barks?

Answer: Pupcorn.

Popcorn on Your Shoulders

Place one piece of popcorn on each shoulder.

Put your hands by your sides.

Don't move your shoulders.

Now **eat** the popcorn without letting it fall to the floor.

Sent in by Kiara N. of Amherst, Massachusetts.

Toe Writing

You will **need** paper and a pen.

Take off your **socks** and **shoes**.

Place a **pen** between your big toe and your second toe.

Now try to **write** your name.

Sent in by Jeff G. of Evansville, Indiana.

Keiko is a real pro at writing with her toes. She can even write a letter this way! Why don't you give it a try?

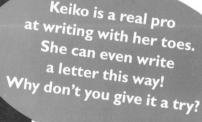

Zfact:

Some birds can do neat stuff with their toes, too. Tree-climbing birds have toes in the shape of an "**x**" with **two toes** in front and **two toes behind**. This allows them to walk straight up or down a tree!

Back-to-Back

Stand **back-to-back** with a partner.
Link both of your arms with the other person's arms.

Then try to sit down and stand back up again **while keeping your arms linked** with your partner's.

Sent in by Reuben and Josh L. of New York City, New York.

Hey, Keiko.

Yeah, Pablo?

Hubow ubare yubou lubikubing thubis bubook subo fubar?

Ubi thubink ubit's lubots ubof fubun! Ubi cuban't wubait tubo subee whubat's nubext!

Nose Strumming

Did you ever wish you had an instrument that you could play like a pro without ever having to practice, an instrument you could carry with you anywhere? Well, you do — your nose!

First **hum** a little tune — any one will do.

While you are **humming,** use a finger to pinch one nostril closed. With another finger, strum your open nostril with a downward motion.

You'll hear a **strumming** sound as the second nostril is closed off and opened up again.

Go ahead and try to play "Mary Had a Little Lamb." Sound good? Try a song from your favorite CD. Grab some friends and form a **nose-strumming band,** or ask people to guess what song you're strumming.

Group Juggling

1 One player **starts** by throwing a bean bag to another player. Then that player throws it to someone else, and so on.

2 The only rule is that every time a certain bean bag comes to you, you have to throw it to the **same person.** This creates a pattern.

Natalie D. of Rural Hall, North Carolina, sent us a letter saying she likes to juggle with her Beanie Babies. Her letter made us think of this zinger.

You will need several different-colored bean bags or Beanie Babies. (The number will depend on the size of your group and how good they are at juggling.)

3 After you've gotten the idea of group juggling down, **add** another bean bag thrown in a different pattern — and another!

Zfacts:

If you think you and your friends are getting pretty good at group juggling, here's a **world record** to go for: According to the *Guinness Book of Records 1996*, in 1994 a group of 826 jugglers kept 2,478 objects in the air simultaneously. Each person juggled at least three objects.

Or maybe you prefer to juggle on your own? If so, **here's another record to consider:** According to *Guinness*, the longest recorded juggling of three objects without a drop lasted more than **11 hours** and **4 minutes.**

Meet Niki and Walter
Two Jammin' Jugglers

Q: Why do you juggle?
Walter: I like to juggle because it's fun and it makes me feel good.

Q: Where do you usually juggle?
Walter: At a juggling club where people practice all kinds of tricks. It helps to watch good jugglers just to see how they move or stay relaxed while they juggle.

Q: Is it hard to learn to juggle?
Walter: Anyone can learn how to juggle. It takes concentration and practice.

Q: What objects do most jugglers like to juggle?
Walter: You can juggle anything, really, but most people juggle balls, clubs, or rings.

Q: Any words of advice you'd like to pass on to jugglers who are just learning?
Niki: Always look at the balls. Don't look down.
Walter: Juggling takes practice and that means dropping a lot of balls.

Now, go out there and juggle!

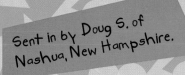
Sent in by Doug S. of Nashua, New Hampshire.

Hands Up!

You will **need** a tennis ball.

Lie down on the floor on your back.

Put a ball between your **feet.**

Now put your arms **over** your head (which means they should be flat on the floor).

Lift your legs and try to **drop** the ball into your hands.

So, David, if you could have something named after you, what would it be?

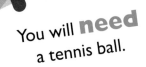

P.S. If you've got this tough zinger licked, here's a new challenge: Keeping your arms straight over your head and the ball in your hands, try to stand up.

A planet.

Dime Dilemma

See page 56 for a hint if you're **zingered.**

Lie on your back.

Place a dime on your nose.

Now try to get the dime **off your nose** without using your hands, moving your body, or turning your head.

Z fact:

The nose can smell about **4,000** different odors!

Sent in by Avi G. of Lexington, Massachusetts.

I can touch my tongue to my nose, so this one is easy for me!

Go Suck on a Lemon

Sent in by Cos T. of New York City, New York.

Try to **suck** on a lemon wedge without making a **sour** face.

Can **you** do it?!?

If you've had enough of sucking lemons and would rather drink lemonade, try this easy recipe.

Lemonade

1¼ cups sugar

½ cup boiling water

1½ cup fresh lemon juice

4½ cups cold water

Ask an adult to help you combine the sugar and boiling water. Stir until the sugar dissolves. Add lemon juice and cold water. Mix well. Chill and enjoy!

Fannee Doolee

loves **food** but hates **eating.** Why do you think that is?

Drops on a Penny

Sent in by Dan H. of Boston, Massachusetts.

You will need:
one penny
an eyedropper
a small bowl or glass full of water

Predict how many drops of water you can fit on a penny.

Then try to **drip** as many drops as possible onto the penny without letting the water overflow.

How many **drops did you fit** on the penny? Challenge your friends to find out who can drip the **most** drops.

Want to learn your fortune with the flip of a coin?
It works like this: A client asks the fortune-teller questions he or she would like answered. Then the fortune-teller tosses two coins to learn the answer.

Both tails up = **Yes**
One tails up and one heads up = **Yes, but it will take some time.**
Both heads up = **No**

P.S. When Lynese did this trick on ZOOM, she fit 43 drops on her penny!

Step Through Your Hands

Clasp your hands together in front of you (with your fingers interlocking). Next, try to **step over** your hands without letting your hands come apart.

Sent in by Michael S. of White Plains, New York.

P.S. If you can't do this zinger, don't worry — it's a tough one! Only half of the cast members could do it.

Here's a joke from Christina S. of Gettysburg, Pennsylvania, that we translated into Ubbi Dubbi.

Hubey, Jubarubed. Whubat dubo yubou gubet whuben yubou cruboss puboisubon ubivuby wubith uba fubour-lubeaf clubovuber?

Ubi dubon't knubow, whubat?

Uba rubash ubof gubood lubuck.

Head-to-Head Spin

Sent in by Danielle and Robert P. of Harrison, New York.

Face your partner.

Next, **kneel** and put your hands behind your back.

Then **bend** over and put the top of your head against the top of your partner's head.

Keeping your heads together, try to **turn** around five times **without** falling down or standing up.

So, Pablo, what kind of animal do you think is most like you?

A wolf.

19

Balloon Bounce

Blow up a balloon.

Without using your hands, see how many times you can bounce the balloon with your head before it touches the ground.

You might also want to try this with a bunch of friends and more balloons.

Sent in by Lindsay A. of Chicago, Illinois.

P.S. You can also try the Balloon Bounce using your knees instead of your head. Try alternating — right knee, left knee.

We interrupt this regularly scheduled book reading for this message from our sponsors:

Lynese: Ub-Hic...ub-hic...ub-hic.

Alisa: Can't get rid of those hiccups? I have a cure — Hiccups Away! Just three spoonfuls of this delightful-tasting syrup and your hiccups will be gone. One, two, three.

[Lynese swallows the syrup and makes a disgusting face.] Her hiccups miraculously disappear.]

Alisa: See?

Lynese: Achoo! Achoo! Achoo! Achoo! Achoo! Achoo!

Alisa: Uh-oh. Back to the drawing board!

[Alisa takes off running.]

Lynese: Achoo! Hey, where are you going? Achoo! What kind of — achoo! — cure is this?

Hang a Spoon from Your Nose

You will **need** a spoon.

Try to **hang** the spoon from your nose.

Invite some friends to do the same.

Remember, **no tape** allowed!

See page 56 for a hint if you're **zingered**.

z fact

According to the *Guinness Book of Records 1996*, the fastest sneeze ever was recorded at 103.6 miles per hour. A sneeze like that during this zinger could be dangerous!

P.S. If you succeed in hanging the spoon from your nose, try walking without letting it fall off.

Walk Through Paper

Here's a challenge:
Make a hole in the paper big enough to fit your entire body through it! Zingered? Think it can't be done? Try this:

You will need:
an 8½" × 11" piece of paper
a pencil
a ruler

Fold the piece of paper in half so that the shorter ends meet.
Draw a line starting at the fold of the paper, stopping an inch from the opposite edge. **Repeat** in the opposite direction, drawing a line toward the folded edge and stopping an inch away. **Keep** drawing lines, like these, in alternating directions all the way to the end of the paper.

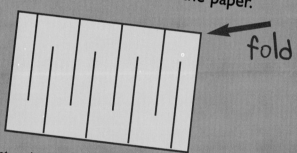

fold

Cut a quarter-inch strip out of the folded edge, starting one inch from the right and ending one inch from the left.

cut out this strip

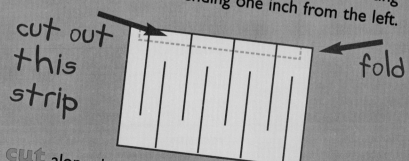

fold

Now **cut** along the lines you made across the paper.
Open up the piece of paper and step through it!

Mysterious Floating Arms

- **Stand in the doorway to a room.**
- **Press the backs of both of your hands against the sides of the doorway for as long as you can stand it (a minute or two).**
- **Then step away and rest your arms down by your side.**
- **Watch as your arms magically float up! They should feel like they're almost weightless.**
- **Put your arms back by your sides and relax. Watch them float up again!**

Sent in by Holly L. of Ionia, Michigan.

Sent in by Noah B. of Manchester, New Hampshire.

What did the judge say when the skonk entered the courtroom?

Answer: Odor in the court!

zfact: IF you were up on the space shuttle, your arms would really float, and so would the rest of you. In space, there is zero gravity. This means you could stand on the ceiling!

24

Don't Lift Your Pencil!

Drawing Games

You will need paper and pencil. Try to draw these figures without lifting your pencil or retracing your lines.

Has your **body** been zingered enough????? Read on and zinger your **brain!**

1.

I have a brain teaser for you. Can you make this shape without lifting your pencil or retracing a line? It's hard for me sometimes.

Zinger #1 was sent in by Molly O. of Longview, Texas.

2.

A B C D E F

3.

Zinger #3 was sent in by Patty N. of Huntsville, Arkansas.

from Thaddeus E. of Georgia.

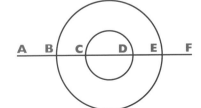

Here's a joke

IF a rooster laid an egg on a roof, would the egg roll left or right?

Answer: Neither. Roosters don't lay eggs!

See page **56** for the answers.

Connect the Dots

Sent in by Noah H. of Longview, Texas.

Draw 9 dots — 3 dots in each row, like this:

Can you connect all the dots by drawing four straight lines?

You must do this **without picking up your pencil,** and **re-tracing is not allowed.**

See page 56 for the answer.

Keiko, who from history or present day would you most like to meet?

Keiko — the whale!

Read a Re [bus]

A rebus is a representation of **words** or **syllables** using **pictures.** Can you read the rebuses below?

See page 56 for the answers.

1. [tie] − e + [hand] − [mountain] =

2. [bone] − one + [ear] =

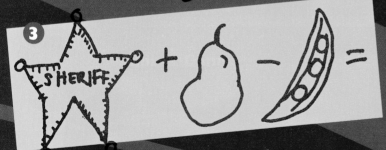

3. [SHERIFF star] + [pear] − [pea] =

Zoops

"My most embarrassing moment was when I was in gym and we were playing T-ball and I kept swinging at the ball that was on the tee but I couldn't hit it. Everybody was laughing at me, even the gym teacher."

— Diana G. of West Newbury, Massachusetts

Decipher the Doodles

Doodle #1 was sent in by Kortne K. of Longview, Texas.

1

2

3 . . . .

4

Fannee Doolee

loves **ZOOM** but hates **TV.** Why do you think that is?

5

6

See page 56 for the answers.

28

Meet David and
Find Out What's Up His Sleeve

Q: How old are you?
David: I'm 8 years old.

Q: How did you get started in magic?
David: I saw a couple of magic shows and that got me interested. Then my dad got me some professional tricks, and I started doing shows.

Q: Where do you perform your magic tricks?
David: I really like doing birthday parties. The guests like to help out, and it's really fun.

Q: Do you ever get nervous while you're performing?
David: When I'm performing, at first I'm nervous. I'm afraid I'm going to do something wrong. But then, later, I just feel good.

Q: Why do you like magic so much?
David: You see a trick and it amazes you because it's like a mystery.

Q: Is there anything else you'd like to say?
David: I hope to see you all at one of my shows!

J

Card Tricks

The Tale of the Three Jacks

Sent in by Karen L. of Chappaqua, New York.

You have to set up the deck before you start the trick. Put the fourth Jack on the bottom of the deck. Do **not** let the other person see you do this!

You will need one deck of cards and a friend. Tell your friend the following story using the deck of cards:

Three Jacks were staying in a hotel. They were best **friends.** *(Flash the three Jacks at the other person and point to the rest of the deck as if it is the hotel.)*

One morning they decided to split up and **meet at noon** for lunch. One Jack went to the top floor of the hotel to take dance lessons. *(Place one Jack on top of the deck.)*

Another went to the basement of the hotel to **swim** in the pool. *(Place the second Jack on the bottom of the deck.)*

The third Jack went to **read a book** at the restaurant in the middle of the hotel, where they were meeting for **lunch.** *(Place the third Jack anywhere in the middle of the deck.)* The clock struck noon. It was time for the Jacks to meet for lunch. *(Ask someone to cut the deck.)*

(Wave your hands over the deck and say "Abracadabra.") Now, let's see if they all made it to lunch. *(Ask your friend to look through the deck and find out.)* They will find the three Jacks **together** in the middle of the deck.

Hint: The only way you might get caught in this trick is if your friend remembers which three Jacks he or she saw. To avoid this, flash the three Jacks quickly in the beginning.

Mind-Reading Card Trick

You will need one deck of cards and a friend.

Shuffle a deck of cards and sneak a peek at the bottom card of the deck. *(Do not let your friend see you do this!)* Tell your friend that you can sometimes **read people's minds** and will prove it with the deck of cards.

Ask your friend to select a card from anywhere in the middle of the deck, **memorize it,** and place it facedown on the top of the deck.

Then ask your friend to **cut the deck.**

Next, pick up the deck yourself. Turn it over and begin **fanning** the cards to the right to look for the card your friend selected. His or her card will be the first card to the right of the original card you peeked at on the bottom of the deck.

If you're doing the trick, you have to remember the card you sneaked a peek at on the bottom of the deck.

According to the *Guinness Book of Records 1996,* the tallest house of cards stood 16 feet high and was 83 card stories tall.

Cards are thin pieces of paper. Why can't we see through them? Card companies coat the cards with a special formula made of china clay, titanium dioxide, castor oil, and other ingredients.

The Queen Tells All

You will **need** one deck of cards and a friend.

Before you start this card trick, **find** all four Queens and put them on top of the deck. (Do *not* let your friend see you do this!)

Facing your audience, **start** four piles — with the four Queens — and keep putting cards on each pile until the deck is gone. It doesn't matter if the stacks are different sizes; in fact, having uneven piles will probably make your trick look even more amazing. (Note: Only you know that a Queen is on the bottom of each pile.)

Ask your friend to take a **look** at the top card in each pile and memorize them. Your friend should *not* let you see the cards.

Tell your friend that you can **read** minds. In fact, you will put all the cards back together into one deck and then mysteriously reveal what was the top card on every pile.

Gather all the piles together, one on top of the other.

Take the top card off the deck, **turn** it over, and say something like "This one's easy because it's already on top. The other ones will be more of a challenge to my mind-reading powers."

With the deck face side up, fan the cards to the right and **look** for the Queens. One Queen will be on the bottom of the deck — ignore this one. The other three will be scattered throughout the pile.

Pull the first card to the right of each Queen — these will be the top cards from each of the piles.

Massage your temples and tell your friend your mind-reading powers are quite exhausted now!

mini crossword puzzle

Here's a joke from Alison T. of Easton, Maryland:

What does a pencil say when someone else is right?

Alison T. - Age 8

Answer: Hmm. You have a point there.

Word Games

You will need

a pencil and paper.

One player suggests a word and **everyone** writes it down. Now, try to make as many **cross-words** as you can in **five** minutes. The one who makes the most **wins.** Let another player pick the word for the next round.

z fact:

According to the Guinness Book of Records 1996, the largest published crossword puzzle was made up of 82,951 squares and contained 12,489 clues across and 13,125 clues down. It covered more than 38 square feet.

We started with the word **ZOOM.** Our mini crossword looked like this:

```
        G
  ZOOM  O
U U     O  OTTER
C C     N  R
C H        LAUGH
H I     INK  I
I N        SUN
N
I
```

33

Pundles

Sent in by Scilla B. and Rowan C. of Arlington, Massachusetts.

Have one person write the following items on a chalkboard or large piece of paper. Then have players guess their meaning.

1. **raSINGINGgin**

2. **thouDEEPght**

3. **Head**
   Heels

4. (**Rosie**)

5. **BAN   ANA**

6. **ME QUIT**

7. **ALL** world

8. **ISSUE**
   ISSUE
   ISSUE
   ISSUE
   ISSUE
   ISSUE
   ISSUE
   ISSUE
   ISSUE
   ISSUE

9. **NAfish**
   NAfish

10. **NME NME NME**
    NME SURROUNDED NME
    NME NME NME NME NME

11. **ME   NT**

12. **HIJKLMNO**

34

More Pundles

If you solved those pundles, try these!

21 FISH

20 BIRD

19 GOOSE

13 monkeying

18 PANTS

14 FISH

17 THRfrogOAT

15 piggy

16 LOCKS
bear
bear
bear

See page 56 for the answers.

Word Wizard

You will **need** paper and pencil.

Write the word
MONSTER
across the top of the page.

Using only the letters in MONSTER, try to make as many **different** words as possible.

The rules: You don't have to use all seven letters in every word. Letters can only be used as often as they appear in the original word. No proper names are allowed.
The **longest** list wins.

We came up with 38 words from MONSTER — try it yourself!

P.S. If you've already conquered **MONSTER** and are still feeling like a word wizard, try a word of your own or any of the following:
HIPPOPOTAMUS, UNFORGIVABLE, or **ANSWER**.

See page 56 for the answers.

z fact:

The largest library in the world is the Library of Congress in Washington, D.C. It holds 28 million books and pamphlets, which are stored on 584 miles of shelves.

Alphabet Nonsense

Can you **make** up a sentence that is 26 words long?

The catch is that the words have to appear in the **order** in which their first letters are found in the alphabet and each word has to start with a different letter.

When you're done, **read** your sentence aloud.

Here's how we got started:

Amy Brewster's cute dog eats frosted granola, huge iced Jell-O kebabs...

Hint: Long lists and lots of adjectives are the key to conquering this zinger.

Zoops

"My most embarrassing moment was when I was at the circus and I went to take a drink of my slush and the straw went straight up my nose. And my best friend told everybody in the front row."
— Mary H. of Concord, Massachusetts

Hink Pinks

Hink Pinks are two one-syllable words that rhyme.

For example, an "obese feline" is a **fat cat.**

Each person is given one of the phrases below and reads it aloud. The group must try to think of the Hink Pink that is synonymous with the phrase.

1. A pile of treats between lunch and dinner
2. Fatigued toes
3. Nonpunctual rendezvous
4. Joker's favorite hat
5. An evening trip through the air
6. A final explosion

See page 56 for the answers.

Now see if you can come up with your own Hink Pinks.

P.S. If you've mastered these Hink Pinks and want a further challenge, try a **Hinky Pinky** (two two-syllable words that rhyme) or a **Hinkety Pinkety** (two three-syllable words that rhyme). Here's a Hinky Pinky to get you started: Rose's strength. (Answer: flower power.)

Sent in by Mike H. and Charlie C. of Mamaroneck, New York.

Guess Ten Body Parts

Try to name ten parts of the body that are spelled with only three letters.

See page 56 for the answers.

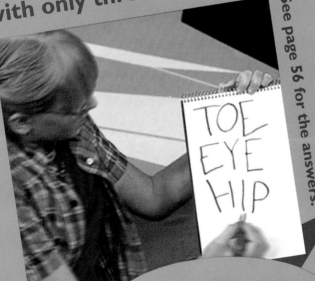

TOE
EYE
HIP

Zfact:

The smallest bone in your **body** is called the stapes or stirrup bone. It is found inside the middle **ear** and is about ⅛ inch long, or about the size of a grain of rice.

So, Zoe, what's the silliest thing you've had to do on **ZOOM?**

I had to read a poem while hanging off a bar. And I couldn't pronounce anonymous. (I still can't say it!)

If you could have someone from history be part of your family, who would it be and why?

"Leonardo da Vinci because I love his art and it touches me, and I want to know who the Mona Lisa was."
— Shari R. of Silver Spring, Maryland

"Berry Gordy because he founded Hitsville USA (Motown)."
— Jayson S. of Washington, D.C.

"A rider from the Pony Express because they were brave."
— Paul D. of Silver Spring, Maryland

"Amelia Earhart because she showed that women are powerful and I believe in that message."
— Sarah R. of Silver Spring, Maryland

"My favorite hero is John Glenn because it was brave of him to go up to space in the first place but to go up to space when he was so old — that's pretty cool."
— Sarah C. of Chestnut Hill, Massachusetts

"Jesse Owens because he could help me run fast."
— Kate K. of Potomac, Maryland

How about you??

Tell your friends that you have magical powers that allow you to see through dice.

- To prove this, ask a friend to toss a die.
- Stare at the die as if you are trying to look through it.
- Then predict the number of dots on the side of the die that is facedown on the table.
- After you've made your prediction, have your friend look at the die to prove you are correct.

Number Games

Dumbfound Them with Dice

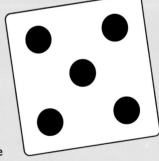

Fortune-tellers sometimes use dice to predict a client's future. Here's how: Using chalk, the fortune-teller draws a Sorcerer's Circle — a circle with a six-pointed star in the middle. Then using his or her left hand, the fortune-teller shakes three dice and tosses them into the circle. Read what dice may say about your future:

One: You will have good health and prosperity for a long time.

Two: You should avoid travel for the next two months and be more considerate of others.

Three: You will have success in love and work.

Four: You will be able to overcome very difficult obstacles.

Five: You will have some hard times but there will be a light at the end of the tunnel.

Six: You will have success in romance.

Note: If two or more dice land outside the circle, the dice are thrown again. If this happens a second time, the fortune-teller warns the client not to make any major decisions and to return in a few weeks. If only one die lands outside the circle, the fortune-teller can proceed. If all three dice land inside the circle, the numbers are added together and take on a different meaning that must be interpreted by the fortune-teller.

What did Cinderella say as she waited for her photos?

Answer: Someday my prints will come.

Puzzling Letters and Numbers

Here are some results from when we tried this puzzle ourselves:

16
sixteen
7
seven
5
five
(4)

7,362
seven
thousand
three
hundred
sixty-two
33
thirty-three
11
eleven
6
six
3
three
5
five
(4)

Give the following instructions to a friend:

Write down any number, but don't let anyone see it. Then, beneath it **write** the same number in words. Next, count the letters in the word or words and write down that **number** of letters. Then write the word.

Repeat this two or more times (more times are needed for larger numbers). As your friend is working through the step above, **astound** him or her by predicting that their final answer will be 4.

Hint: The answer to this puzzle is **always 4**, so it's better not to repeat this trick on the same person or they might catch on to this **pattern!**

42

Eight in the Boxes

You will need paper and pencil.

First, draw a horizontal rectangle.

Next, draw another rectangle over the first one so it looks like a cross.

Then, draw a line through one of the large rectangles.

Count your boxes. You should have eight.

Here's the zinger:

Using a pencil, write the numbers 1 through 8 in the boxes so that no consecutive numbers are touching. For example, the number 2 box cannot touch the number 3 or number 1 box.

See page 56 for the answer.

Sent in by Richard T. of Mesa, Arizona.

1
2
3
4
5
6
7
8

6 + 5 = 9?

Draw six lines like this. They should all be the same length.

Can you **add** five more lines to make nine?

See page 57 for the answer.

| | | | | |

See page 57 for the answer.

Sent in by Gwen G. of Oak Park, Illinois.

Here's a **joke** from Lashonda G. of the Atgeld Murray Community Center/GEM Program of Chicago, Illinois:

What's a cat's favorite color?

Answer: Purr-ple.

So, Alisa, what kind of animal do you think is most like you?

A ferret (one that doesn't smell).

Marvelous Math Prediction

Amaze your friends by predicting the answer to the zinger below. Give the following instructions to a friend:

Choose a number between 1 and 10, but don't say your number out loud.

Double that number.

Add 2.

Divide by 2.

Subtract the original number.

Tell your friend you think their answer must be 1.

Hint: The answer is always 1, no matter which number is chosen at the beginning. So it's better not to repeat this trick on the same person or they might catch on to this pattern!

sum squares

You will **need** paper and a pencil.

Draw a **three-by-three grid** like this, or trace this one:

Using the numbers 1 though 9, **fill in** the grid so that each horizontal and vertical row adds up to 15. You can only **use** each number once!

See page 57 for the answer.

Sent in by Brian O. of Beverly, Massachusetts.

Hubi fubolks.
Subee muby
tubeeth?
Dubon't thubey
lubook grubeat?
Ubi ubused
Ubbi Dubbi
Tuboothpubaste.

Thube tuboothpubaste
thubat mubakes yubou smubile!

Mind Bafflers

Take Me Out to the Ball Game

Five friends are on **five** different softball teams. The teams are the Dolphins, the Cardinals, the Blue Jays, the Cubs, and the White Sox. The five friends' **names** are Catie, Elizabeth, Mary, Kim, and Rosa.

Challenge: Based on the following clues, see if you can figure out **who** is on which team:

- Mary is on the Dolphins.
- Rosa is not on a team with an animal name.
- Elizabeth is not on the Cubs or the Blue Jays.
- Catie's team name has a **u** as its second letter.

Fannee Doolee

loves to play **baseball,** but hates **sports.** Why do you think that is?

The Most Marrying Man in Town

A man married **57** women. None died and he **never** got divorced. And yet he was one of the **most** admired men in town. How could this be?

See page 57 for the answers to these mind bafflers.

Joe watched the circus parade pass by his house.
His mother asked him how many clowns he had seen.
Here's what Joe said:

One clown was in **front** of two clowns.
One clown was **behind** two clowns.
One clown was **between** two clowns.

How many clowns did Joe see?

Clowning Around

The Mysterious License Plate

When Mr. Ollie Lee bought a new car, he asked for a license plate with this number: 33731770.

Can you figure out why he chose these numbers?

33731770

Sent in by Emma S. and Annie B. of Beverly, Massachusetts.

See page 57 for the answers.

The Blue House

There was a one-story house in which everything was blue. **Blue** chairs, **blue** floor, **blue** kitchen, **blue** everything. Now, what color do you think the stairs were?

Sent in by Ariel W. of St. Petersburg, Florida.

Zoops

"My most embarrassing moment was when my friend was up on top of a ladder and we were painting the house, she turned and dropped the paint right on my head. It was green and went all over my clothes."

— Shellie H. of East Falmouth, Massachusetts

48

Something's Fishy Here

Sent in by Christina T. of Laguna Niguel, California.

There were two fathers and two sons. They went fishing and each caught one fish. All together they had three fish. How is this possible?

The Jones Family

Sent in by Jenna F. of Beverly, Massachusetts.

Mary's mother, Mrs. Jones, has four children. The oldest, a boy, she named **North.** The next oldest, a girl, she named **South.** The third, a boy, she named **East.** The youngest child is another girl. What do you think her name is?

See page 57 for the answers to these mind bafflers.

Sent in by Kelly M. of Beverly, Massachusetts.

Shipwrecked

Two boys and their dad are stranded on an island. They have a boat, but it only holds 200 pounds. The dad weighs 200 pounds, and each boy weighs 100 pounds. How will they get off the island if they must all ride inside the boat?

Hint: They can make more than one trip.

49

Other Fun Brain Zingers

Cup Flip

You will **need** three cups.

Put the cups in a **row.**
Then, **turn** the first and third cups upside down and the middle cup right side up.

The goal of this zinger is to make all the cups **face** either up or down.

The rules:

You must flip two cups at a time, and you have to flip the cups a total of three times (no more, no less).

See page 57 for the answer.

Hubere's uba juboke frubom Ubaustubin M. ubof Plubanubo, Tubetubas:
Hubow dubo cubows ubadd uband sububtrubact?

Answer: Wubith uba cubowcubulubatubor.

Just in case your Ubbi Dubbi is a little rusty, we've translated this same joke upside down below.

Here's a joke from Austin M. of Plano, Texas:
How do cows add and subtract?
Answer: With a cowculator.

Paper Clip Chain

Challenge: Make a paper clip chain in midair without touching the paper clips.

You will **need** three paper clips and a one-dollar bill.

Fold the right side of the dollar bill over about a third of the way. Do not crease the fold. **Clip** the two layers of the bill together.

Turn the bill over and fold a third of the other side, still without creasing the fold. **Slide** the second paper clip onto the top of the bill, but clip only two layers together. Both paper clips should frame the number 1 on the front and back of the bill. **Take** the third paper clip and repeat the previous step, placing the clip in the middle of the other two but still only clipping two layers.

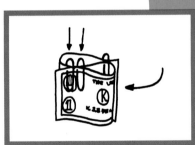

Hold on to an end of the bill with each hand. **Pull!** Your paper clip chain will flip up into the air as it connects.

zfact:

According to the *Guinness Book of Records 1996*, a chain of 190,400 paper clips was made by 60 college students in 5 hours, 50 minutes and measured 18,087 feet long.

Toothpick Test #1

Test #1 was sent in by Sarah L. of Royalston, Massachusetts.

You will need **17 toothpicks**.

Note:
The ZOOMers used pencils because they are easier to see on **TV**.

Set up the toothpicks like this:

Now try to remove only four toothpicks so that four squares are left.

Toothpick Test #2

You will need **12 toothpicks**.

Farmer Ted needs some help. His cantankerous cow, Bessie, knocked down one of the walls of her stall.

See the figure below:

Fannee Doolee

loves the **pool** but hates **water**.

Why do you think that is?

Can you arrange the remaining 12 walls to make six triangular stalls, one for each of Farmer Ted's six cows?

See page 57 for the answers.

Are Your Eyes Playing Tricks on You?

- **Point** at an object in the distance.
- **Close your right eye** and look at the object.
- Then, open your right eye and **close your left eye.**
- Did the object **move** or are your eyes playing **tricks** on you?

The difference you see is because your eyes are spaced apart on your head.

Here are some other ways to test your sense of sight.

1 Which red line is longer?

2 Which is longer — the black line or the red line?

3 Which of the two red lines is longer?

See page 57 for the answers.

Secret to Ubbi Dubbi Revealed...

Hey, Pablo.

Yeah, Keiko?

Would you like to know how to speak ZOOM's secret language, Ubbi Dubbi? Just **add the letters "ub"** before every vowel sound and you, too, can speak Ubbi Dubbi. For instance, if your dog's name is Rover, he becomes Rubovuber. And if your favorite flavor of ice cream is vanilla, it becomes vubanubilluba. Got it? **Grubeat!**

Now go back and see if you can **read** the Ubbi Dubbi in this book — wube wubouldn't wubant yubou tubo mubiss ubout ubon ubanubythubing!

If you have more Ubbi Dubbi questions or want a quick translation, check out the amazing Ubbi Dubbi translator on our Web site at www.pbs.org/zoom. Now you can **ubbify** your e-mail or **dubbify** notes to a friend in mere seconds!

Ubi cuban't bubelubieve wube're ubalrubeaduby ubat thube ubend ubof thubis bubook!

Mube nubeithuber. Ubi thubink Ubi'm guboubing tubo stubart ubovuber ubat thube bubegubinnubing.

54

Who Is Fannee Doolee?

boots

shoes

trees

plants

sweets

candy

oo nn ee

Do you ever wonder who this Fannee Doolee person is and why she's so peculiar?

Why do you think Fannee Doolee likes and hates the things she does? Here's a hint: There is a **pattern** that explains why Fannee Doolee likes and hates the things she does. Fannee Doolee only likes things with **double letters**.

Here's an example: **Fannee Doolee loves sweets but hates candy.** Notice how there are double letters — ee — in sweets but none in candy? Now that you know why Fannee likes and dislikes what she does, why don't you try to **write your own** Fannee Doolee, and send it to ZOOM!

Answer Key

Page 15
Dime Dilemma
Hint: Nose wiggling and face scrunching are permitted.

Page 21
Hang a Spoon from Your Nose
Hint: Try licking or breathing on the spoon before hanging it.

Page 25
Don't Lift Your Pencil!
1. E to A to D to E to C to A to B to C to D.
2. A to B over top to E to D over top to C below to D horizontal to C to B below to E to F.
3. 1. Fold a corner to the middle and draw a dot. 2. Draw a line out from the dot onto the fold. Then draw a circle, stopping only when you reach the fold. 3. Unfold the corner.

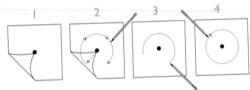

4. Continue the line to complete the circle.

Page 26
Connect the Dots

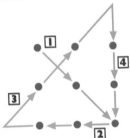

Page 27
Read a Rebus
1. Tiger 2. Bear 3. Badger

Page 28
Decipher the Doodles
1. Boy with long feet wearing a sombrero.
2. Four raisins playing jump rope.
3. Flea jumping contest.
4. Cat chasing a mouse under a rug.
5. Ants carrying a hot dog.
6. Two elephants playing ball.

Pages 34-35
Pundles
1. Singing in the Rain. 2. Deep in thought. 3. Head over heels. 4. Ring around the Rosie. 5. Banana split. 6. Quit following me. 7. It's a small world after all. 8. Tennis shoes. 9. Tuna fish. 10. Surrounded by enemies. 11. Apartment. 12. H_2O. 13. Monkeying around. 14. Starfish. 15. Piggyback. 16. Goldilocks and the Three Bears. 17. Frog in the throat. 18. Ants in your pants. 19. Goose bumps. 20. Bird in a cage. 21. Fishhook.

Page 36
Word Wizard
stone, sermon, snore, store, sore, or, ore, ores, stem, sent, rent, rest, nest, tone, tones, on, one, ones, nose, rose, son, rot, rote, no, not, note, notes, ton, tons, to, toe, toes, some, tome, tomes, roe, eon, eons

Page 38
Hink Pinks
1. Snack stack. 2. Beat feet. 3. Late date. 4. Clown's crown. 5. Night flight. 6. Last blast.

Page 39
Guess Ten Body Parts
ear, arm, hip, leg, lip, eye, rib, jaw, gum, toe

Page 43
Eight in the Boxes

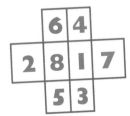

Page 44
6 + 5 = 9?
Add the five toothpicks so that they spell out the word "NINE" as in the figure below:

Page 46
Sum Squares

8	3	4
6	7	2
1	5	9

Pages 47–49
Take Me Out to the Ball Game:
Mary is on the Dolphins; Rosa is on the White Sox; Catie is on the Cubs; Elizabeth is on the Cardinals; and Kim is on the Blue Jays.

The Most Marrying Man in Town:
The man was a priest.

Clowning Around: Three

The Mysterious License Plate: Turn the license plate upside down and it spells "Ollie Lee."

The Blue House: There were no stairs because it was a one-story house.

Something's Fishy Here: There were only three men — a grandfather and his son and grandson.

The Jones Family: Mary

Shipwrecked: The two boys get in the boat and go home. At home, one boy gets out. The other sails back to the island. On the island, he gets out and his father gets in and sails home. His father gets out of the boat and stays at home. Then, the boy at home gets back in the boat and sails back to the island. There, he picks up his brother and they both sail home.

Page 50
Cup Flip
1. Turn over the first and second cups.
2. Turn over the first and third cups.
3. Turn over the first and second cups.

Page 52
Toothpick Test #1

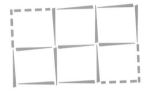

Toothpick Test #2

Page 53
Are Your Eyes Playing Tricks on You?
Take out a ruler and turn back to page 53 to prove for yourself that the answers below are correct.
1. Neither. Both red lines are the same length. The black lines create the optical illusion that the second one is longer.
2. Neither. Both the black and red lines are the same length. The black line only appears to be longer.
3. Neither. Both red lines are the same length. Your brain is tricked into thinking the lower bar is longer because it crosses four lines instead of just two.

Behind the Scenes at ZOOM™

The **Executive Producer** and **Senior Producer** watch a taped show segment of Alisa to decide if they like the way the segment looks on tape. If they don't like it, they will start over again.

Keiko visits one of the ZOOMers' favorite places in the studio!

The Control Room is where the **Assistant Director** and the **Senior Producer** sit and tell the Camerapeople which angles to shoot. The Director picks the camera angle he thinks looks best and then asks the Technical Director, also called the Switcher, to put it on tape.

The **Audio Assistant** puts microphones on the cast members so they can be heard on TV.

The **Makeup Artist** touches up **Pablo's** makeup on the set. The Makeup Artist also does the cast members' hair.

58

Alisa, David, and the **Executive Producer** do some blocking. Blocking is planning how the segment should go — who should be where and when and doing what.

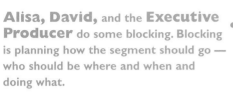

The **Grip,** a **Lighting Operator,** and **Pablo** look on as a segment is being prepared for shooting.

Jared hams it up during a rehearsal.

A **Cameraperson** prepares his equipment for taping.

Keiko, Lynese, and **Zoe** goof off between segments.

A segment with **Alisa** is shot.

A computer controls all the lighting on the set. The **Lighting Operator** controls the lights.

The **Props Assistant** gathers material for the next segment. She helps the **Props Coordinator** get together all the stuff that the ZOOMers handle, including materials for ZOOMdos, ZOOMgames, and ZOOMzingers.

Keiko, Alisa, and **Pablo** chill out during a break.

Each cast member's clothes are kept in a pouch labeled with his or her name. This way **Wardrobe** can be sure that each cast member is wearing exactly the same thing every day — from shirts to scrunchies. This is important because one show consists of a number of different segments that are taped on different days. It would look odd if a cast member's shirt changed from one segment to the next on the same show!

The **Audio Director** sits at the mixing board. This is where microphone volumes are adjusted. The Audio Director can listen to everyone's mic at the same time.

The cast together with everyone it takes to create an episode of **ZOOM**.

Here are some other jobs around the set of ZOOM that you might not know about:

The **Grip** sets up lights and makes shadows.

The **Food Stylist** gets the ingredients ready for the CafeZOOM recipes.

The **Jib Cameraperson** operates a camera that's on a long arm.

The **Drama Coach** makes sure the ZOOMers know how to do all the different things they do on the show.

The **Coordinating Producer** selects which ZOOMgames, CafeZOOM recipes, ZOOMzingers, ZOOMdos, and other stuff are done on the show.

The **Research Assistant** tests the ZOOMgames, ZOOMzingers, ZOOMdos, and CafeZOOM recipes. They're tested at the office and with kids at schools and camps to make sure they work, they're fun, and they're not too easy or too hard.

The **Scenics Technician** builds and moves the scenery.

The **Scenics Carpenter** makes sure that the set is in place and looks the very best for the camera.

The **Post Production Assistant** tracks tapes, segments, and other bits and pieces that help the Editors and Post Production Supervisor do what they need to do. He or she also creates the "Znakes" for the shows, the wiggly names you see on-screen.

The **Production Designer** works on the graphic look of the show, coming up with the logo, set design, and ZOOMerangs.

The **Editor** takes the video footage from the studio shoots and pieces them together with music and graphics to create the final ZOOM shows.

Do you know any ZOOMzingers or other ZOOM material that hasn't appeared on ZOOM?

If so, please e-mail us at www.pbs.org/zoom or write to us at:

ZOOM
Box 350
Boston, MA 02134

If you send us your ideas, you will receive a free issue of ZOOMerang, and we might put your idea on the show! Don't forget to include your first name, last initial, city, and state.

All submissions become the property of ZOOM and will be eligible for inclusion in all ZOOMmedia. That means that we can share your ideas with other ZOOMers on TV, the Web, in print materials, and in other ZOOM ways.

So, c'mon and send it to ZOOM!